Susan B. Anthony

Dona Herweck

Consultant

Timothy Rasinski, Ph.D.
Kent State University

Publishing Credits

Dona Herweck Rice, *Editor-in-Chief*
Robin Erickson, *Production Director*
Lee Aucoin, *Creative Director*
Conni Medina, M.A.Ed., *Editorial Director*
Jamey Acosta, *Editor*
Stephanie Reid, *Photo Editor*
Rachelle Cracchiolo, M.S.Ed., *Publisher*

Image Credits

Cover Bettmann/CORBIS; p.2 Studio_G/Shutterstock p.3 James Steidl/Shutterstock;
p.4 between 1890 and 1910/Library of Congress; p.5 left: argus/Shutterstock; p.5 right:
LC-DIG-ggbain-07590; p.6-7 Stringer/Fotosearch/Getty Images; p.8 left: LC-03122u;
p.8 right: Milos Luzanin/Shutterstock; p.9 The Granger Collection, New York; p.10 left:
Olena Zaskochenko/Shutterstock; p.10 Hulton Archive/Getty Images; p.10 inset: Olena
Zaskochenko/Shutterstock; p.11 top: Bettmann/CORBIS; p.11 bottom: Viktor1/Shutterstock;
p.12 McGuffey, William Holmes, 1800-1873. 2n/Archive; p.13-14 Bettmann/CORBIS;
p.15 top: Bettmann/CORBIS; p.15 bottom: Steve Collender/Shutterstock; rsooll/Shutterstock;
p.16-17 Bettmann/CORBIS; p.18 Bettmann/CORBIS; p.19 top: Bain News Service, publisher;
p.19 bottom: James Steidl/Shutterstock; p.20 LC-3b36893u; p.21 Bettmann/CORBIS;
p.22 left: CORBIS; p.22 right: Bettmann/CORBIS; p.23 LC-USZ61-791; p.24 CORBIS; p.25
LC-DIG-ggbain-30124; p.26 right LC-3b29775u; p.27 top to bottom: LC-3c11870u; Bettmann/
CORBIS; LC-USZ61-791; LC-DIG-ggbain-08785; back cover Steve Collender/Shutterstock

Teacher Created Materials

5301 Oceanus Drive
Huntington Beach, CA 92649-1030
http://www.tcmpub.com
ISBN 978-1-4333-3642-3
© 2012 Teacher Created Materials, Inc.
Made in China
Nordica.092015.CA21501360

Table of Contents

Created Equal

Long ago, on a hillside in **Massachusetts** (mas-uh-CHOO-sits), light flickered from the windows of a cozy farmhouse. Inside the house, eight children gathered near the family fire. They were listening to their father and mother.

"Always remember," their father said, "All people are created **equal**."

"Everyone deserves a chance to work, own a home, and earn a living," their mother added.

"And every adult should be allowed to **vote**," their father finally said.

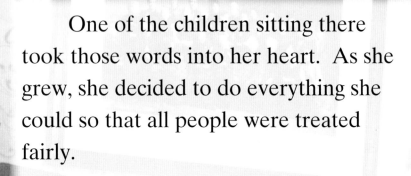

One of the children sitting there took those words into her heart. As she grew, she decided to do everything she could so that all people were treated fairly.

Her name was Susan B. Anthony.

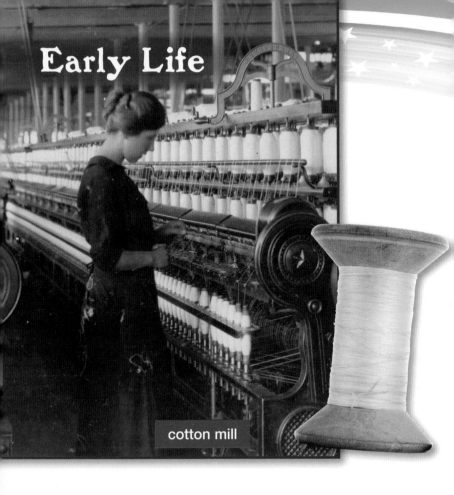

Early Life

cotton mill

Susan Brownwell Anthony was born on February 15, 1820, in the town of Adams, Massachusetts. Her father, Daniel, owned a cotton mill. Her mother, Lucy, cooked, cleaned, and did laundry for the family business.

Quakers

A Quaker is a member of a religion called the Religious Society of Friends. Quakers, or Friends, believe that all people are equal and that God talks to the heart of each person. Quakers got their name because they would sometimes quake, or shiver and shake, with the feeling of God inside them.

The Anthonys were **Quakers**. They led a very simple life. Their home had no decorations, games, or musical instruments. They did not want anything to keep them from thinking about God and what God wanted them to do.

9

Quakers believe in hard work. Susan and the other children had many chores to do. They worked at home as soon as they were old enough to walk and follow directions.

Just one of Susan's chores was making 21 loaves of bread each day!

women and girls
doing daily chores

Education was important to the Anthonys, too. When Susan was four, she and two of her sisters visited their grandfather for six weeks. In that time, their grandfather taught them to read.

Susan's young eyes had a hard time reading for those long hours. The strain seemed to hurt her left eye, and she had problems with it all her life.

McGuffey Readers

Most American children in the mid and late 1800s learned to read with McGuffey Readers. These reading books also taught lessons about right and wrong.

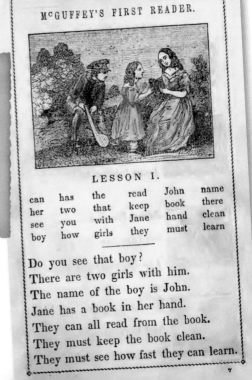

Boarding School

A boarding school is a school where students study and live. The word *boarding* comes from *board* which means to provide meals.

Later, Susan went to a Quaker boarding school in Philadelphia (fill-uh-DEL-fee-uh) to finish her education.

Going to Work

teacher reading
to students

As soon as Susan finished school, she went right to work. She became a teacher in New York in 1839. In those days, very few women worked outside their homes.

a nineteenth-century kindergarten class

While Susan was there, she earned just one-fifth of the pay a man made in the same job. She knew this was not fair, and she said so.

Inequality

During this time, most African Americans were slaves and had no rights. They worked in people's homes and in the fields. They were not considered equal to the people they worked for.

Susan also had friends who were African Americans. At that time, many people thought it was wrong for people of different races to be friends.

Because Susan complained about her pay and had African American friends, she lost her job.

Later, Susan got a better job at another school in New York. People there thought she was a good teacher.

Most women of Susan's age were getting married and raising families. Susan said that she would never marry unless she was given all the rights of any **citizen**. She wanted fair treatment. She wanted the same pay that men got for the same job. And she wanted to vote.

women washing clothes

Florence Jaffray Harriman, Women's Rights activist

"FAILURE IS IMPOSSIBLE"

SUSAN B. ANTHONY

VOTES FOR WOMEN

Temperance

After ten years, Susan stopped teaching. She wanted to do something about the problem of alcohol. She remembered women working at her father's mill who talked about alcohol in their homes. Their husbands would drink and then hurt them and their children. So, Susan decided to work for **temperance**.

temperance
propaganda poster

A Good Friend

In 1851, Susan went to a temperance **convention**. There she met Amelia Bloomer. Amelia was known for shortening her dresses and wearing long, wide pants underneath them. Susan wanted to be comfortable and move around easily. She decided to wear Amelia's style, too.

"**BLOOMERISM**,"
OR THE
NEW FEMALE COSTUME OF 1851,

Amelia Bloomer

22

As it has appeared in the various Citie

BOSTON: S. W. WHEELER, 66 Cornhill—1851.

Bloomers

In those days, women wore only long, heavy dresses to cover themselves completely. Anything else was thought to be improper. Amelia started to change all that. The style of clothes that Amelia wore came to be called *bloomers*.

Elizabeth Cady Stanton and Susan B. Anthony

Susan also met Elizabeth Cady Stanton. They became very good friends. One day their friendship would change women's lives forever.

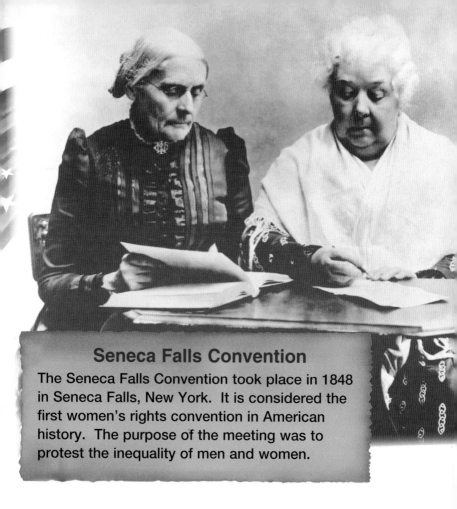

Seneca Falls Convention

The Seneca Falls Convention took place in 1848 in Seneca Falls, New York. It is considered the first women's rights convention in American history. The purpose of the meeting was to protest the inequality of men and women.

In 1852, Susan went to another convention. When she rose to speak, she was told that women could only listen. She was very angry! She decided from that point on to work for **women's rights**.

Susan and Elizabeth worked together. Susan gave speeches around the country that Elizabeth helped to write. She started a paper called *The Revolution* and wrote about women's rights and **suffrage**.

Susan became famous, but the more famous she got, the more some people made fun of her. They laughed at her and called her names. They worked hard to keep her quiet.

Hair Bob

In those days, women almost always grew their hair long and wore it in a bun. Instead, Susan cut her hair in a short bob. Many people made fun of her short hair and bloomers.

Success!

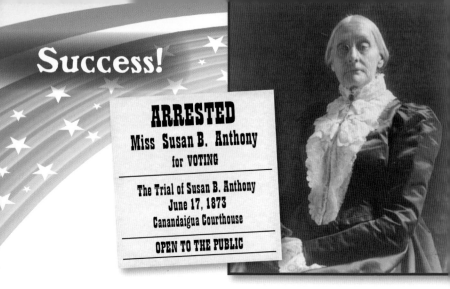

ARRESTED
Miss Susan B. Anthony
for VOTING

The Trial of Susan B. Anthony
June 17, 1873
Canandaigua Courthouse

OPEN TO THE PUBLIC

Susan would not be quiet. In 1872, although it was illegal for women to vote, she voted anyway. She was arrested and went to court. In court, she was not allowed to say anything. She was found guilty and charged a fine, but she would not pay it. The court finally gave up.

When Susan died on March 13, 1906, women in four states had the right to vote. Fourteen years later, the Nineteenth **Amendment** gave all women that right!

Susan B. Anthony Time Line

1820	born in Massachusetts on February 15 ·····
1837	went to a Quaker boarding school
1839	worked as a New York teacher ··········
1848	Seneca Falls Convention
1849	quit teaching and became secretary for the *Daughters of Temperance*
1851	introduced to Elizabeth Cady Stanton by Amelia Bloomer
1852	first public speech at the National Women's Rights Convention
1856	tries to unify the women's rights and African American rights movements
1868	publishes *The Revolution*, a women's rights weekly journal with Elizabeth Cady Stanton ················
1872	arrested for voting illegally in the 1872 Presidential election
1906	dies in Rochester, New York on March 13
1920	Congress passes the 19th Amendment, giving women the right to vote ········
1979	United States honors Susan B. Anthony by issuing a dollar coin with her profile on it

Glossary

amendment—a change in wording or meaning especially in a law, bill, or motion

citizen—a person who lives in a state or country and has all the rights and protection that place allows

convention—a large meeting of people to discuss and learn about a topic

education—learning in school

equal—the same

Massachusetts—a state in the eastern United States

Quakers—the members of the Religious Society of Friends

suffrage—the right to vote

temperance—lowering the use of something to a very small amount

vote—a person's choice for or against something

women's rights—the freedom by law for women to have and do the same things as men are allowed